1

PRAISE FOR
FOODLOOSE

"*Foodloose in Washtenaw* is a celebration of the growing local food movement in Ann Arbor, Ypsilanti, and the surrounding communities in Washtenaw County. Much like *Footloose in Washtenaw* encouraged generations to get out and explore trails through treasured neighborhoods and wilds across Washtenaw County, *Foodloose in Washtenaw* is certain to help folks get to know local farmers and their farms and enjoy the produce of local farms at markets and restaurants across the county. It is a timely and fun guide to Washtenaw County that will certainly deepen our understanding of local culture as related to food."
Robert Grese, Director of Matthaei Botanical Gardens and Nichols Arboretum

"*Foodloose in Washtenaw* has magically interwoven the best elements of sites like Yelp or Local Harvest in a deliciously curated fashion. Landeryou and De Young's snapshot in time of the food scene around Ann Arbor is an unmatched and unparalleled guide to feeling like a local, whether visiting for the first time or having lived here all your life. Their intentionally crafted pocketbook will offer you insights and suggestions to wander through the bounty of the county, enjoying all it has to offer. It's the kind of book that belongs on everyone's shelf. Share it with a friend visiting from out of town, impress your foodie neighbor, or throw it in your backpack and go for a nice weekend bike ride with a loved one. I can only hope to find a Foodloose style guide in every community I visit."
Alex Bryan, Manager of U-M Sustainable Food Program

Published in the United States of America by
Michigan Publishing

DOI: http://dx.doi.org/10.3998/seas.9996999

ISBN 978-1-60785-466-1 (paper)
ISBN 978-1-60785-467-8 (e-book)

CONTENTS

PREFACE

By Taylor Landeryou

We all carry around mental maps in our heads that are based on our past experiences and compiled over time. This mental cartography happens without us being aware of it. But the really cool thing about mental maps is how they serve to help us create and imagine. For example, you have a mental map of your home. You know where the forks are kept, which switch turns on a particular light, and you might even have a pretty good idea of how to get around in the dark. Because of your mental map, you can imagine what it would look like to put a table next to that window, or to hang that picture frame by the doorway. Because of your mental map, you can predict and envision your future. You have mental maps of physical things, but also of concepts. Out of a desire to enrich my mental map of our local food community, I was attracted to the idea of writing this book. The intention is to help you enrich your mental map.

I am a graduate with a MS degree from the University of Michigan School for Environment and Sustainability in the field of Behavior, Education, and Communication. Previously, I studied as an undergraduate at the University of Michigan. As such, I've been living and eating in Ann Arbor for six years. As a freshman, my mental map of the local food community was comprised of the most salient operations, to me, in Ann Arbor. Things like Zingerman's (I didn't know, at the time, there was a difference between the Deli and Roadhouse), the People's Food Co-op, and the Kerrytown Farmer's Market. After attending Local Food Summits, volunteering, and coordinating the Homegrown Festival for several years, my mental map expanded. It was after spending the summer of 2016 working as a production assistant for The Brinery at the Washtenaw Food Hub that my mental map became undeniably enriched with detailed knowledge of connections in our local food community. Now, after writing this book, my mental map comes close to resembling something of a finished product, though, there are of course still things waiting to be uncovered. Which is the beauty of studying this food community, it is ever-changing and allows for new discovery. This book is not a complete reflection of my own mental map, and certainly not of reality, but I think it captures a snapshot of the local food community as it stood in the summer of 2017.

I was particularly drawn to the idea of self-guided tours because I like to think of touring as a practice of re-centering. As Martha Travers, a professor of contemplative studies in the Department of Jazz & Contemporary Improvisation at the University of Michigan imparted to me, it is interesting to think of moving not in a linear direction, but rather in the form of a spiral, which allows us to return and recenter. Every time we have a chance to return to and engage with a place, person, literature, etc., something new can be revealed. There's a relevant quote attributed to Heraclitus that goes "No man ever steps in the same river twice, for it's not the same river and he's not the same man." The food version of which is "you can't eat the same tomato twice" (well, maybe you can, but that's a GMO debate I don't want to invite).

Now, of course, it is not required that you return to exactly where you started, but I would ask that you think about where you are when you start touring: physically, mentally, emotionally, and/or spiritually, and where you are when you stop touring. What has changed? What excited, challenged, and encouraged you? I hope that through these tours we have created a platform from which you can experience awe at the amazing local food community that calls Washtenaw County its home. Perhaps you are inspired to paint some of the beautiful farm landscapes, to pick up local ingredients from a nearby farm market for dinner, or maybe to write a song about your favorite heirloom vegetable. Whatever your medium, I hope that the experiences you have on these tours will encourage you to engage more deeply with your food and the community that creates it.

PREFACE

By Raymond De Young

My wife, Noreen, and I have been long-time students of Washtenaw County's food community. We are Michigan residents since 1977 when, on arrival, I discovered that I have always been a Midwesterner at heart. I also quickly discovered that I was supposed to be a farmer. Thankfully, by working with fine students like Taylor on projects like this one, I have been given a chance to be that farmer.

I've always felt that this part of the country suits the development of long-term relationships to place and people. There are many fine people and places on this planet, but none are better than in this county. Noreen and I settled in Ann Arbor and immediately got involved with the local food community through farmer's markets, the People's Food Co-op, environmental organizations, and, of course, the many fine local restaurants. It took us a bit longer to discover that this county also has a rich and varied agricultural history and a spirit of innovation. Later came the Local Food Summits, Homegrown Festivals, running workshops, volunteering at food banks, gardening everywhere, and attending farm dinners at Green Things Farm. But in-between there was a frightening realization.

My good colleague, Professor Tom Princen, and I are long-time students of community-based responses to environment problems. We read *The Limits to Growth* when it was newly published and have followed Dana Meadows' pioneering work on systems thinking ever since. Over 15 years ago, Tom and I decided to examine the local provisioning system beginning with interviews with the folks who were keeping the older food-related institutions going or innovating new enterprises. In one memorable meeting with the manager of the farmer's market we came to realize how old the average farmer had become and how very few young farmers could be found. Back then, it was very easy to imagine a time in the not too distant future when the market would be greatly diminished and devoid of locally grown food. Thank goodness, that is no longer an easy thing to imagine. But this good outcome wasn't just by chance. In the intervening years many people, working hard, sometimes working alone, often working in groups, on committees, in student projects, and in a dozen other ways, have secured the county's food future. To be sure, it is a type of system and a sense of security that will always be a work-in-progress. But the county is now in a state where a book like this can be written, and future editions imagined.

After that realization, Tom and I did what academics usually do when faced with a problem. We gave talks, ran a seminar, and wrote a book. But the people highlighted in this current book, along with a great many volunteers like my wife Noreen, do the heavy lifting, day after day. They deserve the credit for crafting a vibrant, local-food-literate county. I am always on the lookout for students willing to engage in local, field-based projects with a behavioral focus, like this one. Taylor immediately saw the usefulness of this project and committed her knowledge, time, and attention to making it happen. Taylor created this book's tours and stories that highlight how lucky we are to be in a county with artisan enterprises, food markets, and locally grown goodness. Taylor deserves our deepest thanks. Across all of these individuals and stories she has shown us a new form of pioneer, citizens who are behavioral entrepreneurs.

There are many thanks to offer, most are obvious from the text above. Included are thanks to all the people mentioned in this book, and to all the farm and food folks who aren't mentioned in this edition, but deserve to be in the next. Finally, I thank Wendell Berry for his *Port William* book series on the wonder, pain, hope, and beauty of modern agrarian communities. His American pragmatism reminds us that our responsibility is to the well-being of the soil, animals, and people of a place. For they are the fount of our prosperity.

INTRODUCTION

The idea for this project came from the book <u>Footloose in Washtenaw:</u> *A Walkers' Guide to Ann Arbor and Washtenaw County* (1976) and <u>Footloose in Washtenaw:</u> *A Revised and Expanded Walkers' Guide to Washtenaw County* (1990). Both editions were written by Ruth Kraut and edited by Keith Taylor. These books provide self-guided walking tours of the county, sometimes trails and other times sidewalks. The book you are currently reading is intended to be the food version; hence food instead of foot. The idea is to capture the 2017 Washtenaw County local food community in the form of self-guided tours. These tours are curated with the hope of encouraging those not explicitly connected to the food community to get to know our food community more intimately and to become involved, perhaps by volunteering at one of the many sites described.

Foodloose attempts to weave the multitude of connections that abound between farmers, restaurants, retailers, and other members of the Washtenaw County local food community into tours that allow for the understanding of the larger patterns at play. We encourage asking questions about geography, social networks, shared experiences, and more that might reveal what makes our local food community so unique and worthy of celebration. Then, we can begin to ask what is missing from our community, or what could improve it? These tours are based on simple connections, such as geographical proximity, themes, or simply following a flow of food. Many intricate inter-relationships exist that have not been included in this book and you are invited to discover for yourself some of these intricacies and uncover your own connections.

There are biases of this book that are not entirely representative of the local food community. Some of the most apparent biases include how this book has a focus on vegetarian as well as organic, pesticide-free, and biodynamic food ventures. The information for this book was gathered through interviews that were traveled to by bicycle, bus, and the occasional car ride. This limited the scope of the project to within county boundaries. It is unfortunate that some folks who engage with our local food community were not included because they are not geographically located within Washtenaw County; nonetheless, their work is still extremely important to us.

Additionally, some of the tours in this book involve spending money at some point, in some way. It is important to recognize that it might not be possible (or wise) for some tour-goers to purchase something at every stop on a tour. For this reason, some of the tours, such as Tour de Farm and Lil Piggy's Markets do not require spending money to have an experience. However, people who grow, process, cook, and distribute our food should have their time and effort honored with compensation. Although, their compensation does not necessarily have to be money. Money is, of course, the most convenient method of transaction, but only because we have made it so. We can, in fact we once did, exchange goods and/or services without using money. Humans have so much more to offer than greenbacks or plastic. We have skills, we have experience, we have time, and we have the ability to reciprocate creatively. This book encourages you to find a way to exchange your skills with someone who has food skills, in order to use your actions, not your money. In doing so, you will be fostering a meaningful connection with someone in your community as well as the food you eat.

As Frida Kahlo once said, "Nothing is absolute, everything changes, everything moves, everything revolutionizes, all flies and goes." This flux exists within our local food system. A farm, store, or restaurant featured in the book will close and others will open; some already have. Due to the constraints of a published book, this single edition cannot reflect this cycling. Thus, the book you are currently reading is a snapshot of the Washtenaw County local food community. It does not claim to be comprehensive, nor does it claim to be the ultimate guide to our county's local food. It is simply a curated set of tours that encourage a certain way of exploring the food community based on how it stood in 2017. If you are looking for more information about local foods, check out the Further Readings section of this book.

Another reason something/one might have been omitted was because of time constraints in the interview process. Summer is generally a busy time of year for food folks, so finding a moment to spare is rare. A "call-out" was posted in several locations around the county describing how interested and relevant parties could get in touch. Some local food operations did not meet the guidelines, which is another potential reason for omission. The main guideline was that the food operation was physically located in Washtenaw County. Further, they needed to demonstrate how they partner with a couple of other local food enterprises in the county. How many "a couple" meant was determined relative to the scale of operation; the bigger the operation, the more partners they were asked to demonstrate.

When reading this book, you might notice that not all points on the tours have a Feature page. Operations that were specifically interviewed for this book have such a page. Other points are included because they fit nicely within the tours. These points are not in the gray boxes on the Addresses page. There are three symbols you will find throughout the book that designate 1) a confirmed public restroom, 2) Wi-Fi, and 3) places to sit, eat, gather, etc.

WI-FI   PLACES TO GATHER   REST ROOMS

Starting at Whitney Farm on Jennings Rd, you will continue to Joy Rd and pass Sunseed Farm on the left. Once you reach Whitmore Lake Rd, turn right. The Joy House Hens egg stand will be on your left and on your right is the Slow Farm's U-Pick and Ark of Taste field. A little further down Whitmore Lake Rd, the Washtenaw Food Hub is on your right. This could serve as a resting point halfway through the tour.

Next you will turn left onto Warren Rd until you reach Pontiac Trail (it begins to curve here). Take a left and a little less than a mile down Pontiac Trail you will find the big red barn of the Tilian Farm Development Center on the right. Continue on Pontiac Trail and turn right on Nixon Rd. Over a mile down on Nixon Rd and after you cross over Warren Rd, Green Things Farm will be on your right. Turn around and take a left on Warren Rd and a little ways down you can find Seeley Farm on your left. Take Warren Rd back to Whitmore Lake Rd and take a right to return to the Washtenaw Food Hub.

This map is not drawn to scale.

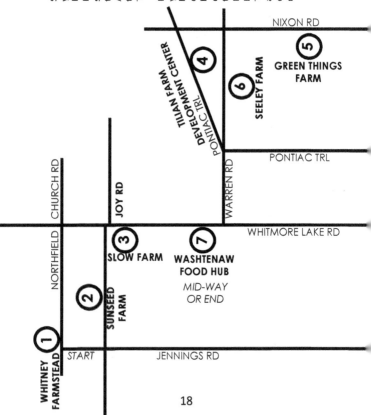

18

TOUR DE FARM

This tour was based off of a conversation that Taylor had with her fellow Piscean and former boss, David Klingenberger, owner of The Brinery. He recalled a faint memory of bicyclists touring the grouping of farms near the Washtenaw Food Hub on Whitmore Lake Road. When interviewing and researching for this publication, Taylor spent a majority of the time on her bicycle traveling from farm, to restaurant, to farmer's market, etc., so you can imagine the concept of a bicycle tour piqued her interest, especially one that included views of beautiful farms just outside the city of Ann Arbor. Hopefully, we can organize an actual Tour de Farm soon for the whole community to participate in and engage with, but even when there isn't an established event happening, this bicycle tour is still accessible! It is important to note that we ask on the farmer's behalf that you **do not enter the farm properties without consent of the farmer**. These are working farms that are not set-up for tours. Please, simply admire their beauty from the road. If you are interested in getting to know the farm/farmers, you can get in touch with them in-person at farmer's markets, over email, or via phone.

If you are starting from the city of Ann Arbor, one of our favorite routes to get to the farm is to bicycle along the Huron River, past the cascades, over the dam, and through Bandemer Park onto Whitmore Lake Road. However, heading North on Whitmore Lake Road is pretty difficult on bicycle because it is a gradual uphill the entire way, and there isn't an established bike lane. If this doesn't float your goat, we recommend taking Pontiac Trail, which has a bike lane (most of the way) and a less demanding incline to Warren Road and then to Whitmore Lake Road. You can also take an Ann Arbor bus most of the way along Pontiac Trail (consult The Ride Guide), with your bike stowed on the front of the bus. You get off the bus at the stop before Dhu Varren Road and then bike the rest of the way. Of course you can also drive for this tour and in that case, we recommend starting on Whitmore Lake Road.

From Whitmore Lake Road, take a left onto Northfield Church Road which eventually (about 3 miles) curves right and becomes Jennings Road, on your left you will pass the beautiful, centennial **Whitney Farmstead**. Turnaround, go back through the Northfield Church Road curve, then turn right heading South down Jennings Road for about a mile. Turn left onto Joy Road, you will pass **Sunseed Farm** on your left about half way to Whitmore Lake Road, 3 miles in total. Take a right on Whitmore Lake Road and you will pass the **Joy Road Hen's** roadside stand (from which you can purchase eggs) and ride alongside a portion of **Slow Farm** that is home to the **Pig Gig** on the left hand side of the road, further down on your right is the U-Pick and Ark of Taste field of **Slow Farm**.

A little ways down Whitmore Lake Road you will pass the **Washtenaw Food Hub**. This stop could serve as a half-way point if you need to refuel or to take a break. It can also serve as a beginning point for the second portion of the tour. From here you will turn left onto Warren Road until it meets up with Pontiac Trail. Take a left onto Pontiac Trail and less than a mile down the road on your right is a big red barn. This is the **Tilian Farm Development Center.** Continue on Pontiac Trail until it connects with Nixon Road (about a mile), which you will take a right on. A mile down the road on the right, just past Warren Road, will be **Green Things Farm**. Turnaround and head back towards Warren Road and take a left. Watch out for baby painted turtles on this road. Taylor saw two crossing when she was biking through one sunny, July day. A little over half a mile down the road on your left is **Seeley Farm**. The folks from Seeley Farm and Green Things Farm incubated together at Tilian Farm Development Center. Farmers, neighbors, friends, community – this is what it's all about and what inspired this book. Continue on Warren Road to Whitmore Lake Road, take a right and head back to the Food Hub.

You have officially toured de farms!

WHITNEY FARMSTEAD

5525 JENNINGS RD, ANN ARBOR, MI 48105

SLOW FARM

4700 WHITMORE LAKE RD, ANN ARBOR, MI 48105

TILIAN FARM DEVELOPMENT CENTER
4400 PONTIAC TRL, ANN ARBOR, MI 48105

GREEN THINGS FARM

3825 NIXON RD, ANN ARBOR, MI 48105

WASHTENAW FOOD HUB

4175 WHITMORE LAKE RD, ANN ARBOR, MI 48105

SUNSEED FARM
5000 BOYDEN DR, ANN ARBOR, MI 48105

SEELEY FARM
2150 WARREN RD, ANN ARBOR, MI 48105

WHITNEY FARM STEAD

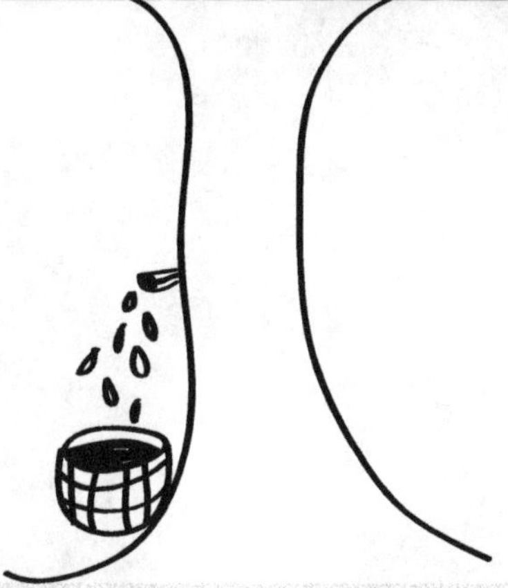

Whitney Farmstead was established in 1900. Five generations later, it is now being stewarded by Malaika Whitney and Matthew Haarklou. When Taylor visited with them, Malaika was harvesting garlic scapes and Matthew was working with one of their friends to construct the foundation of what would soon be their milking parlor. They raise a variety of pasture animals and collect the sap of maple trees to produce maple syrup. Their sugar shack is pictured on the left. Every year, around the end of winter and beginning of spring, they host a Pancake Supper and Open House so you can check out their taps and trees. In the meantime, you can find Malaika and Matthew and their products at the **Ann Arbor Farmer's Market**, **Cobblestone Farmer's Market**, and **Argus Farm Stop**. In addition to maple syrup, they offer Herd shares, beautiful Agrarian Cards, Pastured Pork, a Winter Meat CSA, Wool, and 100% Grass-fed Lamb and Beef.

5525 Jennings Rd. Ann Arbor, MI 48105

whitneyfarm.squarespace.com

facebook.com/whitneyfarmstead

SLOW
FARM

Slow Farm spans across Whitmore Lake Road and US-23. Nestled amongst these two high-speed roadways, this farm offers a place to truly slow down and enjoy local food. When we talked with Kim Bayer about this book, she was heading out to the farm later that day to plant an "Ark of Taste" garden near the U-Pick Strawberries which aims to preserve heirloom food varieties. This year, the farm featured U-Pick asparagus, strawberries, pumpkin, and squash with Peter Brauer leading the operation. Peter also farms Abby's Acres Chickens at **Tilian Farm Development Center**. Slow Farm was also a home to the **Pig Gig,** a collaboration between Angela Martin and Jae Gerhart. One of their delightful pigs is pictured on the left. For the tour, visit the U-Pick field; depending on the time of year, you can pick yourself some local goodies!

4700 Whitmore Lake Rd. Ann Arbor, MI 48105

slowfarmandfriends.com

facebook.com/slowfarmandfriends/

TILIAN FARM
DEVELOPMENT
CENTER

Tilian Farm Development Center is a farm incubator that is home to a variety of farming operations such as honeybees, year-round greens, eggs, and heirloom varieties. You can find farmers from Tilian at most of the area Famer's Markets. The farmers of Green Things and Seeley got their start at Tilian and are now located just around the corner. Farmers at Tilian use open fields, hoop houses, and there's even an old camper for some hens. There is also a vermicomposting system that was established by Jesse Raudenbush, similar to other systems he has set-up in the area. Biking past the farm on Pontiac Trail you can catch glimpses of the hens and of the old magnificent barn, but if you want to stop by to tour the farm, and maybe help with some weeding, they have visiting hours 12-6 PM on Sundays. However, it is best to contact them in advance.

4400 Pontiac Trail Ann Arbor, MI 48105

tiliancenter.org

facebook.com/pg/tilianfarm/about

GREEN THINGS FARM

GREEN THINGS FARM

Green Things Farm, despite their name, offers some not so green things such as flowers, pigs, cattle, and chickens. You can meet the Green Things farmers at the Ann Arbor Farmer's Market or stop by their farm stand. The stand is open from Thursday evening to Sunday evening, July through Thanksgiving. Additionally, they host weekly community outdoor farm dinners July through September. You can sign-up for these dinners on their website in early summer (sign up early as they fill up fast). The dinners feature local food and music as well as a chance to tour the farm. Nate and Jill Lada started this farm as a part of their training at the **Tilian Farm Development Center** in the spring of 2011 and found their own plot of land in 2013. Like many of the farms in this area, they are improving the land they steward by using restorative and ecologically-sensitive agricultural practices, and it seems to be working since their things are pretty green.

3825 Nixon Rd, Ann Arbor, MI 48105

 greenthingsfarm.com

facebook.com/Green-Things-
Farm-194011453965755

WASHTENAW
FOOD HUB

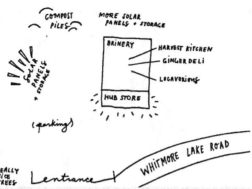

The **Washtenaw Food Hub** is home to **The Brinery** and serves as a production space for **Locavorious**, **Harvest Kitchen**, and **Ginger Deli**. It is owned by Richard Andres and Deb Lentz of **Tantré Farm**. The best way to tour the hub is to check out the hub store, which at the time this book was written was under construction. The store promises to showcase prepared foods crafted from nearby farms and the processors mentioned above. The hub also has several solar panel arrays. In the past the site was a feed and fertilizer supply store, which might explain its relatively central location among Ann Arbor farms. Thus, it can serve as the beginning, a place to take a break in the middle, or as the last stop on the Tour de Farm, it just depends on how long you prefer to tour. Just like the farms, the food hub is a place of work, so we ask on behalf of the "hubbers" that you do not enter the property except to visit the hub storefront (when it is open).

4175 Whitmore Lake Rd, Ann Arbor, MI 48105

 washtenawfoodhub.com

facebook.com/washtenawfoodhub

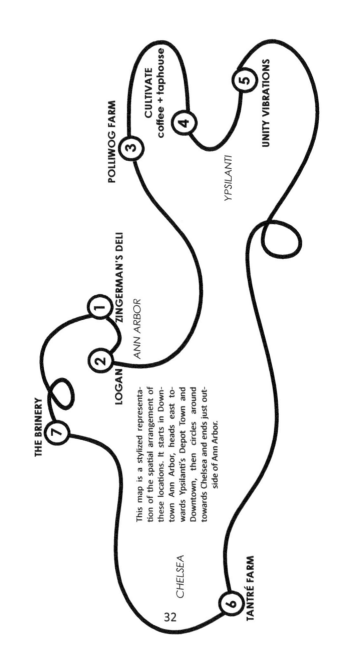

POLLIWOG FARM

CULTIVATE
coffee + taphouse

③

④

⑤

UNITY VIBRATIONS

YPSILANTI

ZINGERMAN'S DELI

①

②

ANN ARBOR

LOGAN

THE BRINERY

⑦

This map is a stylized representation of the spatial arrangement of these locations. It starts in Downtown Ann Arbor, heads east towards Ypsilanti's Depot Town and Downtown, then circles around towards Chelsea and ends just outside of Ann Arbor.

CHELSEA

32

TANTRÉ FARM

⑥

DEGREES OF SEPARATION

After describing the idea for this book to Kathy Sample of **Argus Farm Stop** she said "Oh, like Six Degrees of Separation," which is a comparison we had not previously considered. However, Taylor thought "hey, like why not?" Kevin Bacon's name is food-related AND he was in *Footloose* (1984)*, there are so many connections, how could we not create a tour named this? Thus, this tour is based off of the idea that these food points are all connected by six degrees (or fewer) of separation to each other, not to Kevin Bacon, at least to our knowledge that is.

*FULL DISCLOSURE: we have never seen *Footloose* (1984) and don't really know anything about Kevin Bacon, we just googled him.

We start off with **Zingerman's Delicatessen** in Kerrytown and then head just off of Main Street to **Logan** restaurant. For 10 years, Thad Gillies was the Executive Chef of Zingerman's Delicatessen and he is now the Executive Chef of Logan. In many of his dishes, Chef Thad serves the delightful micro greens of this tour's third location, **Polliwog Farm**. Polliwog Farm products are also served at **cultivate coffee & tap house**, the fourth point on this tour, located in Ypsilanti's Depot Town. Just outside of downtown Ypsilanti, is the **Unity Vibration Kombucha Beer and Tea Brewery and Triple Goddess Tasting Room**. In addition to countless stores and their tasting room, you can find Unity Vibration kombucha on tap at cultivate. Unity Vibration's Farm-to-Barrel kombucha batches take us to the sixth location of this tour, **Tantré Farm**. Tantré Farm's many fruit-bearing trees and bushes provide ingredients for these locally-inspired kombucha varieties and they also supply cabbage and production space to **The Brinery**. David Klingenberger, The Brinery's owner, spent many years as a farmer at Tantré. The Brinery brings us full circle as they ferment Tantré cabbage into sauerkraut which is then an essential ingredient in the Deli's sandwich, the #2 Zingerman's Reuben.

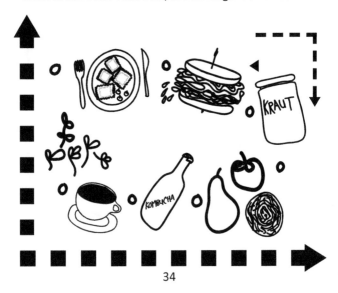

LOGAN

115 W WASHINGTON ST, ANN ARBOR, MI 48104

CULTIVATE COFFEE & TAP HOUSE

307 N RIVER ST, YPSILANTI, MI 48198

TANTRÉ FARM

2510 HAYES RD, CHELSEA, MI 48118

ZINGERMAN'S DELICATESSEN
422 DETROIT ST, ANN ARBOR, MI 48104

POLLIWOG FARM

N PROSPECT RD, SUPERIOR CHARTER TWP, MI 48198

UNITY VIBRATION

93 ECORSE RD, YPSILANTI, MI 48198

THE BRINERY

4175 WHITMORE LAKE RD, ANN ARBOR, MI 48105

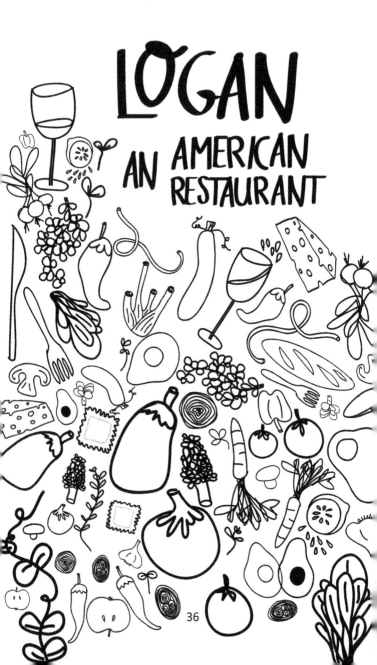

LOGAN

AN AMERICAN RESTAURANT

Logan restaurant in downtown Ann Arbor is inspired by the chic dining experiences one might have in New York City or Chicago. However, Logan offers something that's not on the menu in any New York or Chicago dining establishment, ingredients grown in Washtenaw County of course! They source produce from the **Ann Arbor Farmer's Market**, **Argus Farm Stop**, and, in particular, the micro greens of **Polliwog Farm**. Chef Thad's brother runs a permaculture farm in the area from which they also source ingredients. Moreover, all of the organic waste matter from the restaurant is recycled by the farm's compost system. On a historical note, the space Logan now inhabits was once home to one of Ann Arbor's well-known gay bars, **The Flame** (sign pictured top left, Photo Credit: Jim Rees).

115 W Washington St, Ann Arbor, MI 48104

 logan-restaurant.com

facebook.com/logan.americanrestaurant/

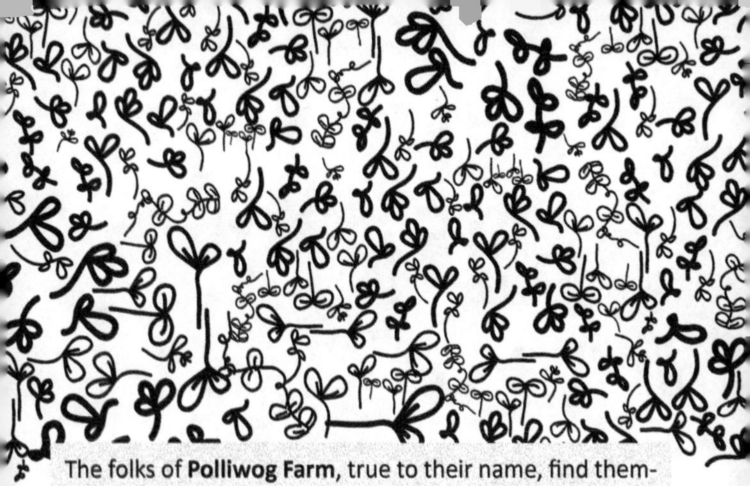

The folks of **Polliwog Farm,** true to their name, find themselves inhabiting the transition between two ways of living. In a world that seems indifferent to the plight of nature, these farmers maintain a sensitivity and compassion for the environment and the communities they are partnered with. In addition to their family farm, they also work with Dawn Farm, an addiction treatment center. They specialize in microgreens, but offer several other products which you can find at **Ollie Food + Spirits,** **Ypsilanti Co-Op, Depot Town Farmer's Market,** and the next stop on our tour, **cultivate coffee + tap house.** Polliwog Farm welcomes visitors, but ask that you please get in touch with them in advance.

Prospect Rd, Superior Charter Twp, MI 48198

polliwog.farm/

facebook.com/PolliwogFarm/

dawnfarm.org

The three C's of **cultivate coffee + tap house** are *craft*, *community*, and *causes*. It was designed with the intention of creating a space where community members can gather, support each other, work together, and enjoy a variety of beverages and treats. Which includes the kombucha beer and tea of **Unity Vibration**. This space also features an outdoor garden, the produce of which, is donated to local food pantries and organizations committed to ending hunger. You can check out their websites for current information on the multitude of daily/nightly, weekly, or montly events they host. These events include things like board game nights, music, yoga in the garden, and various meetups.

307 N River St, Ypsilanti, MI 48198

cultivateypsi.com/

facebook.com/cultivateypsi/

What was once a glass-making factory and then a hang out spot for a biker club is now the **Unity Vibration Triple Goddess Tasting Room and Brewery**. Located on the east-side of downtown Ypsilanti, this award-winning brewery offers a variety of rotating kombucha beers and teas. It started as an operation out of Rachel and Tarek's home and is now distributed nationwide. Although their kombucha can be found across the country, they brew many beers and teas that are flavored from ingredients found in our county. They have a farm-to-barrel series that features produce from nearby farms such as **Tantré Farm** and **Black Locust Gardens**. Besides their work in the local food community, they also support the arts community of Ypsilanti by serving as one the venues for the First Fridays monthly arts & culture walks.

93 Ecorse Rd, Ypsilanti, MI 48198

unityvibrationkombucha.com

firstfridaysypsi.com

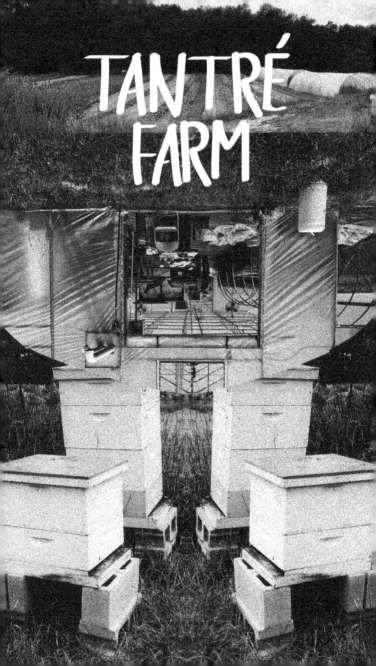

Tantré Farm located in Chelsea, Michigan is an organic farm owned by Richard Andres and Deb Lentz. Although it is a small, family-owned farm, this is one of the larger and older farms in the area. In addition to their CSA shares, they sell their produce at the **Ann Arbor** and **Chelsea** farmer's markets. Although they specialize in produce, they tend to livestock such as chickens, pigs, and bees. Each growing season they like to experiment with a few items and try out new or intriguing varieties. In addition to several acres of fields, they use hoop houses to extend their seasons. One of the truly unique aspects to this farm is the mushroom log forests where they cultivate a few species of edible fungi, including shiitake. Deb was once a school teacher and enjoys giving tours of the farm to school groups. Like many of their fellow farmers, they welcome volunteers, just be sure to get in touch with them in advance. On Fridays, the farm hosts pizza dinners for CSA members which is a wonderful and delicious opportunity to get to know the farm and the farmers.

2510 Hayes Rd, Chelsea, MI 48118

tantrefarm.com

facebook.com/Tantre-Farm-117468354932495/

The Brinery preserves all sorts of local produce through the ancient art of fermentation. They offer several kinds of fermented food items such as sauerkraut, kimchi, hot sauce, and seasonal pickled produce (think ramps and nettles in the spring, cucumber dill in late summer). They source their produce from many area farms including **Tantré Farm** and **The Dyer Family Organic Farm**. The Brinery is the anchor tenant of the Washtenaw Food Hub. Looking at the impressive production facility now, it's hard to imagine that the owner of The Brinery, David Klingenberger, got his start making sauerkraut by hand on a picnic table. Many more hands (all still local) are involved in the production of these fermented goods. You can find The Brinery products on the menu at many local restaurants and on the shelves of almost every grocery store in the county (and beyond). If you want to meet the Brine Wizards in person, check out their stall at the **Ann Arbor Farmer's Market; please do not go to the production facility** . The photo to the left features sauerkraut being brined. Photo credit: Patrick Record.

thebrinery.com

facebook.com/TheBrinery

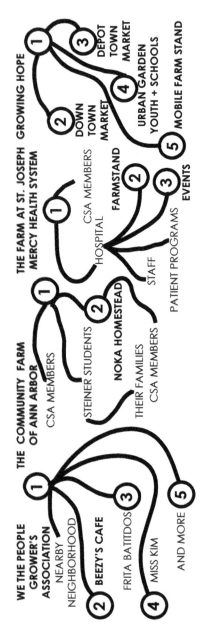

WE THE PEOPLE GROWER'S ASSOCIATION
THE COMMUNITY FARM OF ANN ARBOR
THE FARM AT ST. JOSEPH MERCY HEALTH SYSTEM
GROWING HOPE

1 NEARBY NEIGHBORHOOD
2 BEEZY'S CAFE
3 FRITA BATIDOS
4 MISS KIM
5 AND MORE

1 CSA MEMBERS
2 STEINER STUDENTS

NOKA HOMESTEAD
THEIR FAMILIES
CSA MEMBERS

1 HOSPITAL
CSA MEMBERS
FARMSTAND
2 EVENTS
3 STAFF
PATIENT PROGRAMS

1
2 DOWN TOWN MARKET
3 DEPOT TOWN MARKET
4 URBAN GARDEN YOUTH + SCHOOLS
5 MOBILE FARM STAND

This diagram maps out some of the connections of the four featured operations. The numbers have no significance, they are just used for organization. You can tour each operation and it's connections as a tour or you can tour different points from each operation. Choose your own adventure.

FARM TO TABLES

This tour takes a closer look at four farming operations that bring farm-fresh food to many tables in our community. These four farms stood out to us because we found that while they had many connections within the local food community, their operations go beyond food. Their focus is on whose tables the food will find its way to. What's interesting is that each of these farms has a different approach.

There are several ways to take this tour. You could visit each of the farms as its own tour. Another way to go about it might be to focus on a farm, try to dive in, and follow its food. For example, you could coordinate to volunteer for a day at the Community Farm of Ann Arbor and then head to the Ann Arbor Farmer's Market to say hello to your new farming friends at the market stall. Finally, you could check out NOKA Homestead's stall at the Dexter farmer's market. The head farmer of NOKA got her farming start at the Community Farm of Ann Arbor and Tantré Farm.

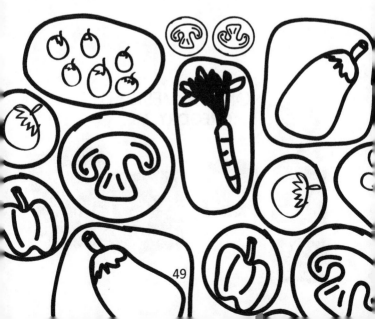

49

WTPGA 1301 S HARRIS RD, YPSILANTI, MI 48198	**COMMUNITY FARM** 1525 S FLETCHER RD, CHELSEA, MI 48118
THE FARM AT ST. JOES 5557 MCAULEY DR, YPSILANTI, MI 48197	**GROWING HOPE** 922 W MICHIGAN AVE YPSILANTI, MI 48197

NOKA HOMESTEAD
GREGORY, MI

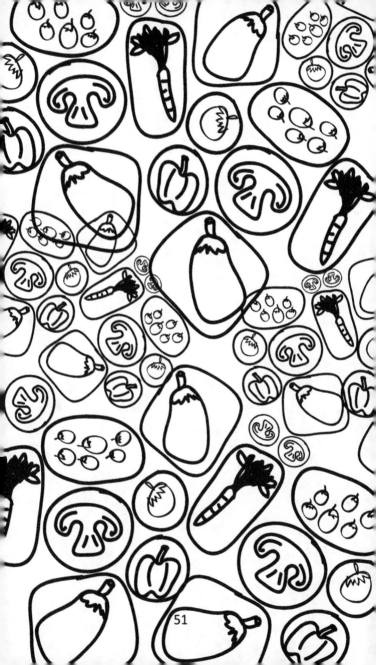

WE THE PEOPIE THE GROWER'S ASSOCIATION

After spending time with Farmer Melvin Parson, it was easy to see the vast impact this farm is having not just at area restaurants, but also within the neighboring community. For example, Farmer Parson refers to the children that live across the street as the "Green Veggie Eaters" because they enthusiastically eat the vegetables grown on the farm. At many restaurants in both Ypsilanti and Ann Arbor, such as **beezy's cafe**, **Frita Batidos**, and **Zingerman's Roadhouse**, you will find produce from **We the People Grower's Association** gracing the tables. After the experience of tending to a friend's gardening plot and realizing the need to have people that look like him growing and selling food, Melvin started this farm. He had a connection with Pastor Powell of the Grace Fellowship Church House of Solutions and is now farming in the southeast corner of their property. Melvin started this season with seedlings from **Green Things Farm**. He envisions creating a world-class urban farm in Ypsilanti over the years to come.

1301 S Harris Rd, Ypsilanti, MI 48198

wethepeoplegrowersassociation.com

facebook.com/We-the-People-Growers-Association-601247606643549

THE COMMUNITY
FARM OF
ANN ARBOR

The main farmer of **NOKA Homestead**, previously worked as a farmer for **The Community Farm of Ann Arbor**. Taylor spent half a day on this farm working alongside the crew and she came to understand the mutualistic relationships the farmers have with their CSA members. In fact, several members of the crew that day were also CSA members. The farm's tractor was converted from a fossil fuel guzzler to a fully solar-powered machine by two of the CSA members. In addition to the members, they also host an annual trip from the Steiner School's 9th grade class which allows the students to experience local, community-supported agriculture. The Community Farm of Ann Arbor is known as the first CSA in Michigan, it has paved the way for the thriving population of CSA operations in this area. In addition to produce, they tend to several goats, an apiary of honey bees, and a cow named Lucy.

1525 S Fletcher Rd, Chelsea, MI 48118

 communityfarmofaa.org

facebook.com/communityfarmofannarbor

THE
FARM AT
SAINT
JOSEPH
MERCY
HEALTH
SYSTEM

One doesn't usually think of a hospital campus as the setting for a farm, but **The Farm at Saint Joseph Mercy Health System** has shown, that with a little imagination, amazing work can be done. Being located in such proximity to the hospital allows The Farm to access many tables that are not as easy for traditional farms to reach. Think of bedside tables and pregnant women's plates, the places that could really benefit from having healthful food. What impressed me the most about this farm was the Eisenhower Center's hoop house designed to facilitate rehabilitation for brain-injury patients; this truly encompasses the concept of healing through farming. The Farm also serves CSA members from the hospital staff and nearby neighborhoods. In addition to the hospital community, they connect with the general public through their weekly farmstand as well as annual events they host, such as the Luminary Walk.

5557 McAuley Dr, Ypsilanti, MI 48197

 stjoesannarbor.org/thefarm

facebook.com/stjoefarm

GROWING HOPE

Similar to the other farms featured in this tour, **Growing Hope** is more than just a farm. It is an organization dedicated to serving the community. Growing Hope organizes the weekly **Ypsilanti Downtown** and **Depot Town Farmer's Markets**. They also operate a mobile farm stand that travels around the area with fresh, local food. They cultivate an urban farm in Ypsilanti and partner with multiple youth and school farming programs. Growing Hope also hosts many events throughout the year at their urban farm. For example, the *Chefs in the Garden* series celebrates local food through artisan meals prepared by notable local chefs such as Brandon Johns of **Grange**, Andrew Stevick, and Eve Aronoff of **Frita Batidos**.

Photo credits to the Growing Hope Staff.

922 W Michigan Ave, Ypsilanti, MI 48197

growinghope.net

facebook.com/growinghope

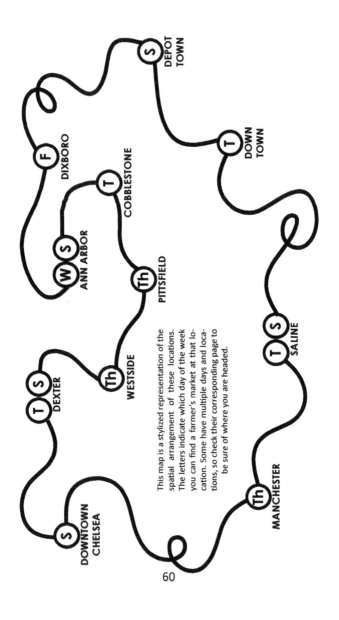

This map is a stylized representation of the spatial arrangement of these locations. The letters indicate which day of the week you can find a farmer's market at that location. Some have multiple days and locations, so check their corresponding page to be sure of where you are headed.

DEPOT TOWN — S

DIXBORO — F

DOWN TOWN — T

COBBLESTONE — T

ANN ARBOR — W S

PITTSFIELD — Th

SALINE — T S

DEXTER — T S

WESTSIDE — Th

DOWNTOWN CHELSEA — S

MANCHESTER — Th

LIL PIGGY'S MARKETS

No more "this lil piggy went to market, this lil piggy stayed home", because all of the lil piggys are going to all of the markets! Although Saturdays are often considered *the* farmer's market day, Washtenaw County offers farmer's markets almost every day of the week during the summer months. Plus, there is an impressive number of markets that continue through the winter months.

For this tour, you can take several routes. You might start by picking a day of the week and making an effort to visit all of the farmer's markets on that day. Another option would be trying to visit at least one market each day of the week. We weren't able to find farmer's markets on Sundays or Mondays, but you can visit places like Argus Farm Stop (see the Liberty St. Foodie Legacy tour) or the local food co-ops in Ypsilanti or Ann Arbor. They all offer local farmer's fresh produce. In Washtenaw County it is truly possible to make a visit to a farmer's market a part of your daily routine. Depending on where you start from, you can bicycle between some of the markets. You can also take the city buses, although some of the markets are not on bus routes; it might be easier to access them by carpooling. Get your baskets ready to be filled with local and seasonal treats and treasures and get your mouths ready to chat with all the farmers!

TUESDAY

COBBLESTONE

2781 PACKARD ST, ANN ARBOR, MI 48108
4-7PM, MAY-OCTOBER

YPSILANTI DOWNTOWN

16 S WASHINGTON ST, YPSILANTI, MI 48197
3-7PM MAY-OCTOBER
WINTER: INDOORS, SAME LOCATION THRU DEC.

DEXTER

3238 ALPINE ST, DEXTER, MI 48130
2-6PM, MAY-OCTOBER

SALINE

7265 ANN ARBOR-SALINE RD, SALINE, MI 48176
3-7PM, JUNE

WEDNESDAY

BUSHEL BASKET

1010 S MAIN ST, CHELSEA, MI 48118
2-6PM, MAY-OCTOBER

ANN ARBOR

315 DETROIT ST, ANN ARBOR, 48104
7AM-3PM, MAY-DECEMBER
FIRST WEDNESDAYS FOOD TRUCK RALLY, MAY-OCT

& FRIDAY

DIXBORO

5221 CHURCH RD, ANN ARBOR, MI 48105
3-7PM, MAY-OCTOBER

THURSDAY

PITTSFIELD TOWNSHIP

6201 W MICHIGAN AVE, ANN ARBOR, MI 48108
3-7PM, JUNE-SEPTEMBER

WESTSIDE

2501 JACKSON RD, ANN ARBOR, MI 48103
3-7PM JUNE-SEPTEMBER

MANCHESTER

209 ANN ARBOR ST, MANCHESTER, MI 48158
3:30-7PM, MAY-OCTOBER

SATURDAY

ANN ARBOR

315 DETROIT ST, ANN ARBOR, MI 48104
7AM-3PM, MAY-DECEMBER,
WINTER: 8AM-1PM, JANUARY-APRIL

CHELSEA

128 PARK ST, CHELSEA, MI 48118
8AM-1PM, MAY-OCTOBER,
WINTER: 500 WASHINGTON ST, NOV-APRIL

DEXTER

3233 ALPINE ST, DEXTER, MI 48130
8AM-1PM, MAY-OCTOBER,
WINTER: 7720 ANN ARBOR ST, JANUARY-APRIL

SALINE

7265 ANN ARBOR-SALINE RD, SALINE, MI 48176
8AM-NOON, MAY-OCTOBER,
WINTER: 9AM-NOON, OCTOBER-APRIL

YPSILANTI DEPOT TOWN

100 RICE ST, YPSILANTI, MI 48197
9AM-1PM, MAY-OCTOBER,

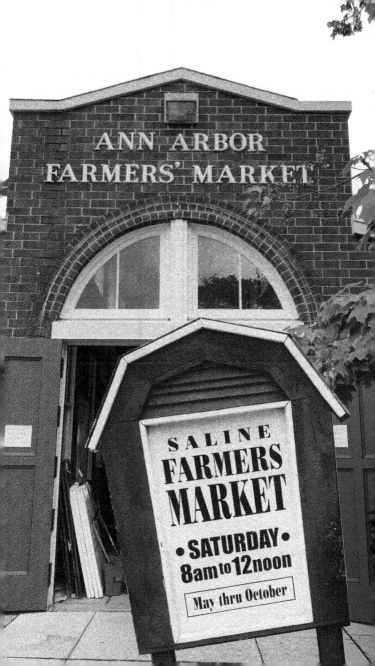

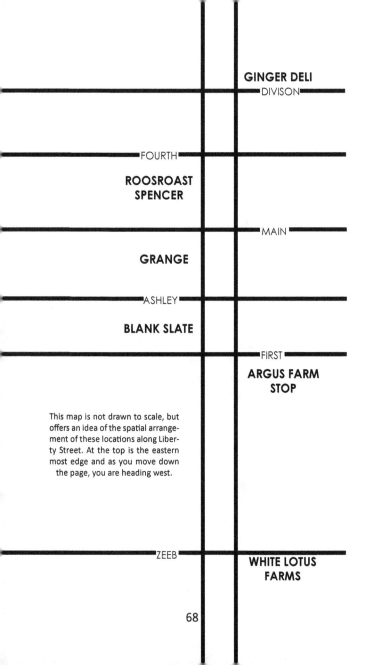

GINGER DELI

DIVISON

FOURTH

**ROOSROAST
SPENCER**

MAIN

GRANGE

ASHLEY

BLANK SLATE

FIRST

**ARGUS FARM
STOP**

This map is not drawn to scale, but
offers an idea of the spatial arrangement of these locations along Liberty Street. At the top is the eastern
most edge and as you move down
the page, you are heading west.

ZEEB

**WHITE LOTUS
FARMS**

LIBERTY ST.
FOODIE
LEGACY

In the past few years, Liberty Street in Ann Arbor has had an influx of local food endeavors settle along it. This street, particularly the blocks near Main Street, has been and continues to be home to many food and drink-related businesses. **Grange Kitchen and Bar** inhabits 118 W. Liberty St, which according to the Ann Arbor Historic District Commission*, is part of the historic Adam and Anton Schaeberle Buildings (112-122 W. Liberty). This collection of buildings was occupied in the mid-1880 by a harness shop, a meat market, flour and feed shop, a shoe store, and a saloon. **Alley Bar**, which is located at 112 W. Liberty St, was occupied by Binder's Saloon around 1880. Across the street, at 111 W. Liberty St, **Vin Bar** currently inhabits what was, from 1880-1892, the Ludwig Walz Grocery and Saloon. As you explore all that Liberty Street has to offer, we invite you to also consider its food-related past.

For this tour, we envision spending a day on Liberty Street, but of course you can also break it up over a week, lunar cycle, season, year, or even a lifetime! Taylor spent several years of her life living just off of Liberty Street and still never tires of it. Ray and family once lived on North Main street and remember walking past all these sites as the local food movement took root. We have formatted this tour around the traditional meal times of breakfast, lunch, and dinner but we welcome any add-ins such as afternoon coffee or late-night ice cream.

* Historic Buildings: Ann Arbor, Michigan Second Edition by Marjorie Reade and Susan Wineberg Second Printing, 1998. Copyright 1992 by the Ann Arbor Historical Foundation and the Ann Arbor Historic District Commission

BREAKFAST

If it is a Saturday in the summer, we recommend starting way out West at **White Lotus Farms**. They offer an à-la carte market of cheese, bread, produce, pastries, and even pizza from 9:30 AM – 1:30 PM. If it is not a Saturday, start your day off at **Argus Farm Stop** on West liberty with a beverage from their cafe and your choice of toast from the fresh breads they offer. Local food community member, Kim Bayer, advised Taylor on this "toast hack".

LUNCH

Ginger Deli is the spot for all your Bánh mì and Phở needs. If it is a Thursday in the summer, we recommend you to check out the Bank of Ann Arbor's Sonic Lunch, a free concert series hosted at Liberty Plaza just across Division Street from Ginger Deli. A short walk away, you can stop in at **RoosRoast Coffee Works** for coffee, obviously, and some lighter snacks, most of which are locally sourced.

DINNER

Long-standing farm-to-table restaurant **Grange Kitchen and Bar** is one option for a market fresh dinner paired with artisanal cocktails. **Spencer** is another dinner option with delightful wine and cheeses as well as an ever-changing menu, perfect for sharing. If you have room for gourmet ice cream, then **Blank Slate Creamery** should be the next stop on your tour.

WHITE LOTUS FARMS

7217 W LIBERTY ST, ANN ARBOR, MI 48103

ARGUS FARM STOP

325 W LIBERTY ST, ANN ARBOR, MI 48103

GINGER DELI

303 S DIVISION ST, ANN ARBOR, MI 48104

GRANGE

118 W LIBERTY ST, ANN ARBOR, MI 48104

\
ROOSROAST COFFEE WORKS
**117 E LIBERTY ST, ANN ARBOR, MI 48103
&/OR ROSEWOOD ST, STE B, ANN ARBOR, MI
48104**
\
SPENCER
113 E LIBERTY ST, ANN ARBOR, MI 48104
\
BLANK SLATE CREAMERY
300 W LIBERTY ST, ANN ARBOR, MI 48103

White Lotus Farms is known for their bread, cheese, croissants, and goats. You can find them at many of the area farmer's markets, or you can go to them. On Saturday mornings they open the farm up for CSA members to pick up their shares and for the general public to check out their a la carte market. They set up market carts in a little corner of the farm with one cart for cheese, one for bread and produce, another for beverages and ordering fresh pizza, and then you pay for whatever you pick out at the end. In addition to all of the delightful food, you can check out their beautiful goats and fluffy bunnies. The farm itself is covered with gorgeous willow trees and you can walk around some of the gardens and raised beds. One of our favorite things to see is the massive and mesmerizing koi pond. Visiting White Lotus Farms is a great way to spend a Saturday morning — especially if you have kids or if you just want to bring out your inner child!

7217 W Liberty St, Ann Arbor, MI 48103

whitelotusfarms.com

facebook.com/WhiteLotusFarms

ARGUS
FARM STOP

What was once J.B. Sunoco gas station and mechanic shop is now **Argus Farm Stop** at 325 West Liberty. They refer to themselves as an everyday farmer's market, but we might describe it as a farm consignment shop. The cafe portion of the store supports the operating costs. The business is organized so that the farmers earn about 80% of the profit as compared to less than 20% in regular grocery stores. In addition to all of the seasonal produce, Argus has some diverse offerings, including foraged food, uniquely prepared food items, and artisan products like salves and cards. Cafe customers can use the Wi-Fi and have access to several indoor and outdoor seating locations. They recently added a greenhouse structure onto the West Liberty store, which is used for cafe seating as well as meetings and events. Folks have even gotten married there! At the time of this book's publication, a second Argus Farm Stop location has opened on Packard Street.

325 W Liberty St, Ann Arbor, MI 48103
also
1200 Packard Rd, Ann Arbor, MI 48104

argusfarmstop.com

facebook.com/argusfarmstop

Ginger Deli, a popular lunch spot, is located on the corner of Liberty and Division across from Liberty Plaza in downtown Ann Arbor. They serve Vietnamese cuisine such as Bánh mì and Phở with several vegetarian-friendly options. You place an order at a window, through which you can spot the shelves of baguettes waiting for their turn to become beautiful Bánh mìs. There is some outdoor seating that consists of picnic tables and cafe-style tables. During the colder months, they enclose and heat an area around the order window which offers seating as well. Ginger Deli uses some of the industrial kitchen space at the **Washtenaw Food Hub**. Taylor recalls the day the owners of Ginger Deli came by to tour the hub, She was shredding peppers to make hot sauce at **The Brinery**. In addition to the restaurant, they offer catering and lunchboxes for events. Ginger Deli also serves as a recurring guest restaurant to the University's hospital cafeteria.

303 S Division St, Ann Arbor, MI 48104

gingerdeli.com

facebook.com/Ginger-Deli-1387801301444657

Chef Brandon Johns of **Grange Kitchen and Bar** says "if you want pork, you need a pig". This won't surprise you if you've seen his brilliant tattoo of a pork cuts chart. He and his restaurant have been serving up local cuisine for almost a decade. Located in what was at one time a butcher shop, they are proud to continue the legacy by butchering their own locally-sourced meats. They use produce from the **Ann Arbor Farmer's Market** and have partnered with many farms in the area, such as **Seeley**, **Green Things,** and **Tantré**, to name just a few. In addition to their cuisine, they are known for their artisanal cocktails. Additionally, Chef Johns has been featured in **Growing Hope's** *Chefs in the Garden* series.

118 W Liberty St, Ann Arbor, MI 48104

 grangekitchenandbar.com

facebook.com/grangekitchenandbar

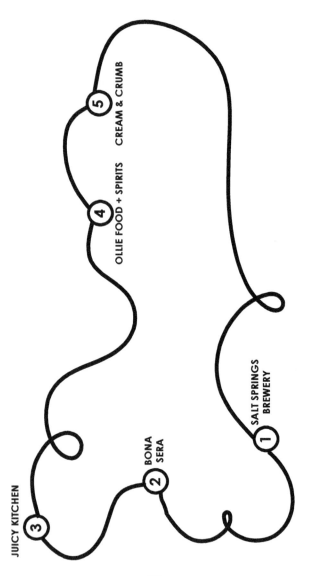

1. SALT SPRINGS BREWERY
2. BONA SERA
3. JUICY KITCHEN
4. OLLIE FOOD + SPIRITS
5. CREAM & CRUMB

FOODIE FINDS

Taylor has never really considered herself to be a "foodie" (although, after writing this book she might need to reconsider), nor did we "find" any of these places. However, we do like food and have found that alliterations in titles are quite catchy, so there you have it. After living in Washtenaw County as a student for six years (Taylor) and as a student and faculty member for 38 years (Ray), we've had our fair share of family and friends visit. Generally they wish to go out to a restaurant for dinner, brunch, etc. at some point during their stay. The purpose of this meal, besides nourishment, is to get a feel for this area through food.

We have found that after a few such visits, it can be a challenge to come up with anything original, reasonably priced, and/or convenient to access. If you're like us, you will feel an enormous pressure to take visitors to cool spots, but ones that you haven't dined at too recently. And, of course, there's always the issue of if you're "in the mood" for a certain kind of dining experience. Like most folks, we have our own list of places to take out-of-towners. This tour includes some of the new joints we have recently discovered and have added to our lists. The hope is that they get added to yours. Now, if you don't have a list of places to take visitors, consider this a starting point.

We have these restaurants labeled in an order, but we do not think it is necessary to follow that order. This tour is intended to be taken over a longer time period. Maybe you end up checking out a place every time someone visits, or perhaps on each full moon you try one of these restaurants. However you decide to go about it, use it as an opportunity to open up to something new. Additionally, we've included a local-food-neighbor to each restaurant for you to check out while you are there.

SALT SPRINGS BREWERY

117 S ANN ARBOR ST, SALINE, MI 48176

BONA SERA

200 W MICHIGAN AVE, YPSILANTI, MI 48197

JUICY KITCHEN

1506 N MAPLE RD, ANN ARBOR, MI 48103

OLLIE FOOD + SPIRITS

42 E CROSS ST, YPSILANTI, MI 48198

CREAM & CRUMB

44 E CROSS ST, YPSILANTI, MI 48198

WHAT IS **YOUR** FOODIE FIND?

PLEASE SHARE IT WITH US:
**2034 DANA, 440 CHURCH ST
ANN ARBOR, MI 48109**

USE THIS SPACE TO REMEMBER THE NAMES OF
YOUR FINDS

Salt Springs Brewery in Downtown Saline is the first stop on this tour. It is located in an old church that they lovingly renovated. They have maintained the magnificent stained-glass windows and added a marvelous, and hilarious – we think even Michelangelo would get a kick out of it – ceiling mural. They source their food ingredients from **The Brinery** and several farms of the **Tilian Farm Development Center** in addition to the **Ann Arbor and Saline Farmer's Markets**. Besides serving delicious and seasonal local food, they have a large selection of craft brews. As if the church interior wasn't enough, there is also an outdoor area. In the warmer months, they have live music in the outdoor space which is complete with both formal and informal dining areas, a large fire pit, and a bar. It is right across from the Saline Farmer's Market and within walking distance of **McPherson Local**. The latter is a local shop that carries basics like milk and eggs and, in addition, more specialty items like macaroons, homemade hummus, and other artisan goods.

117 S Ann Arbor St, Saline, MI 48176

 saltspringsbrewery.com

facebook.com/saltspringsbrewery

BONA SERA.

Bona Sera in Downtown Ypsilanti is a wonderful spot for dinner as well as weekend brunch. They have unique fare that incorporates both Southern (United States) and Italian cooking traditions. Many of their dishes feature seasonal and foraged ingredients with the owner foraging many of the mushrooms used in their dishes. The space is also a showcase for local artwork as part of Ypsi's First Fridays event series. Below the restaurant, there is an underground space that hosts many gatherings and events throughout the year. Just up the street is **beezy's cafe**, a great lunch spot that sources from **We the People Grower's Association**.

200 W Michigan Ave, Ypsilanti, MI 48197

eatypsi.com

facebook.com/bonaserarestaurant
facebook.com/bonaseraunderground

Tucked away in a small plaza on Ann Arbor's West Side is **Juicy Kitchen**, a cozy breakfast and lunch spot with a delicious and healthful menu. Some of the locally sourced food items they serve are **RoosRoast Coffee Works** coffee, **Polliwog Farm** greens, and **The Brinery** products. We're huge fans of their seasonally-inspired quiche. Although the menu is mainly vegetarian, you can easily have them add meat products (e.g., bacon, chicken sausage) to your order. They have many vegan and gluten-free options as well. In the warmer months, they have outdoor seating. A few doors down, in the same plaza, is **El Harissa Market Cafe**. This cafe specializes in North African and Mediterranean cuisine. And if you are feeling inspired from your cafe meal, you can purchase ingredients and spices from the same regions in the market section.

1506 N Maple Rd, Ann Arbor, MI 48103

juicykitchen-a2.com

facebook.com/Juicy-Kitchen-169930263052607
facebook.com/El-Harissa-Market-Ca-
fe-637223529656064

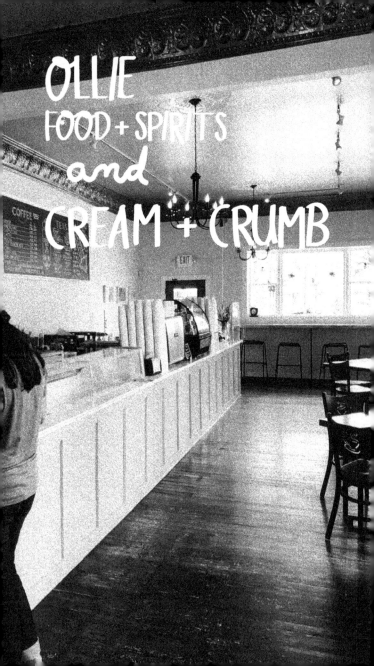

For the fourth and final stop on this tour, head over to Ypsilanti's Depot Town for dinner and dessert at **Ollie Food + Spirits** and **Cream & Crumb**. The locally-sourced food dishes by Chef Travis Schuster are complemented by the seasonal cocktails. For dessert, they offer a selection of **Zingerman's** pastries, **Hyperion Coffee**, which is roasted about a block away, and Guernsey Farms ice cream. Out back there's a lovely patio for enjoying a meal or treat during the pleasant weather months. All sorts of local food spots are within walking distance. There's the **Ypsilanti Food Co-op**, **cultivate coffee + taphouse**, and the **Depot Town Farmer's Market** on Saturdays.

42 E Cross St, Ypsilanti, MI 48198
44 E Cross St, Ypsilanti, MI 48198

ollieypsi.com
creamandcrumbypsi.com

facebook.com/OllieYpsi
facebook.com/CreamandCrumbYpsi

ACKNOWLEDGMENTS

We are so grateful to all the members of the Washtenaw County local food community. Without you, this book would not be possible. Thank you for your strong commitment to local food. To everyone that agreed to let us interview them during the busiest season, thank you so much for handing over some of your valuable time, it is greatly appreciated.

To everyone that encouraged this project, we appreciate you! Thank you Jason Colman for guiding us through the publishing process. Alex Bryan, we are grateful for all of your advice and support. Ruth Kraut, thank you so much for meeting with Taylor and also being cool with us applying your books' concept to food. Keith Taylor, your reassuring words helped us navigate the editing process with ease. Phil and Lora Myers, thank you for your generous contribution to the editing process. Delia Mayor, thank you for offering your nimble editing skills. Kim Bayer, thank you for being such an unwavering advocate of our local food community and for your heartfelt advice on writing this book.

Finally, we thank our families for their endless support and encouragement.

FURTHER READINGS

Taste the Local Difference, Magazine
(localdifference.org)

Edible WOW, Magazine
(ediblewow.ediblecommunities.com)

Footloose in Washtenaw: *A Walkers' Guide to Ann
Arbor and Washtenaw County* (1976) and Footloose
in Washtenaw: *A Revised and Expanded Walkers'
Guide to Washtenaw County* (1990) by Ruth Kraut,
edited by Keith Taylor

The Unsettling of America: *Culture & Agriculture* by
Wendell Berry

LOCAL: *The New Face of Food and Farming in
America* by Douglas Gayeton (a recommendation
from Kim Bayer)

The Localization Reader: *Adapting to the Coming
Downshift* edited by Raymond De Young and
Thomas Princen

Slow Food Huron Valley, local organization
(slowfoodhuronvalley.com)

Local Food Summit, annual event
(localfoodsummit.org)

CPSIA information can be obtained
at www.ICGtesting.com
Printed in the USA
LVHW02s2345290418
575353LV00024B/158/P